Stop Smoking

The Factors That Initially Led Me To Take Up Smoking
And The Subsequent Process Through Which I Overcame
My Reliance On Tobacco

*(The Most Simplified Approach To Permanently Ceasing
Cigarette Consumption)*

Fernando Dudley

TABLE OF CONTENT

Introduction 1
An Invitation To Embrace A Distinctive Way Of Living 4
Stomach Relaxing..22
Benefits Of Smoking Cessation On Health 26
Utilize All The Available Assistance At Your Disposal..52
Phytotherapeutic And Naturopathic Solutions For Smoking Cessation 55
Manage And Regulate Your Emotions........................67
Smoking Is A Habit 79
What Got You Hooked...89
The Potential Advantages To One's Health Resulting From The Practice Of Tobacco Consumption...........95
Coughing Up Blood..129
Benefits Of Giving Up Smoking For Your Health And Mental Well-Being 140

Introduction

We're not trying to scare or discourage you. However, these are the unpleasant facts which accompany the practice of smoking. Scholarly investigations have demonstrated that smoking has ramifications beyond the individual smoker, as individuals subjected to second-hand smoke may be at greater risk of developing lung cancer compared to active smokers themselves. It is not surprising that a significant number of individuals are endeavoring to cease the aforementioned habit. Nonetheless, it must be highlighted that the pivotal term in this context is 'attempting'. Majority of individuals who smoke experience significant difficulty in relinquishing their habit.

What is the reason for the difficulty being experienced? The reason behind this phenomenon can be attributed to the presence of nicotine, a chemical substance inherent in tobacco, that induces a sense of elevated mood or euphoria similar to potent drugs such as cocaine, heroin, and amphetamines. Consequently, corporations and medical professionals have devised substitutions for traditional cigarettes, such as nicotine transdermal patches, with the intention of mitigating an individual's withdrawal symptoms subsequent to their abandonment of the habit of smoking. Additional viable options encompass electronic cigarettes, nicotine aerosols, and nicotine troches. These products evoke a sensation of relaxation akin to smoking, while being devoid of the health hazards associated with cigarette smoking. However, it is frequently observed that remedying a smoking addiction necessitates more than a readily available commercialized item.

To successfully cease smoking, a collaborative endeavor among the smoker, their loved ones, and appointed healthcare experts is imperative. The addictive potential of nicotine is widely recognized, rendering the process of quitting cessation difficult for many. However, please do not despair as achieving the task at hand is certainly possible. As a matter of fact, multitudes of individuals have successfully accomplished the act of smoking cessation by acknowledging the detrimental effect of smoking on their health and undertaking measures to quit the habit. Similar to any other addiction, periodic manifestation of withdrawal symptoms may occur. However, it is important to not excessively criticize oneself during the instances when these symptoms prevailed and prompted one to resort to smoking. This is normal. Nevertheless, there are individuals who are capable of quitting abruptly. A word of caution: This particular approach may not be suitable for everyone and could potentially result in severe withdrawal symptoms that may persist for a significant period of time. However, this approach frequently represents the optimal strategy to maintain abstinence.

An Invitation To Embrace A Distinctive Way Of Living

We have resumed our travel on the bus, and are en route towards your prior residential area where you initially began your smoking habit. It is my utmost pleasure to assist you in navigating towards the conveniently located Easy Exit Off Ramp. In this regard, may I draw your attention to certain aspects of your former haunt (smoking enclave?) that you appear to have overlooked or possibly not given sufficient consideration during your residency?

Primarily, as per the National Drug Survey, it is a widely acknowledged fact that ninety percent of individuals who smoke have initiated the same either at the age of eighteen or prior. Half of them commenced at the age of fifteen or earlier. It is likely that you initiated smoking at a relatively young age. The act of smoking is a habitual practice that was often initiated during childhood through fleeting moments, thereby becoming a lifestyle for many individuals.

During the initial client consultation, I typically inquire about their age of initiation for smoking. Upon being informed, I proceed to inquire humorously, "Did an individual wield a firearm in your presence?"

Regrettably, a young man responded in the affirmative by stating, 'Indeed, to some extent.' I initiated smoking during my tenure as a soldier in Iraq. Additionally, some have shared their experience of adopting smoking as a means to cope with hazardous or distressing situations. The concept of universality does not apply universally.

However, the majority of us would likely answer negatively, as there was no external coercion to speak of. We engaged in it as a jest, attempting to appear sophisticated, endeavoring to mature, and aspiring to be part of the popular group. For many individuals, their immediate family members, such as parents, siblings, or even close acquaintances, were habitual smokers. The practice of smoking was imbued in our lifestyle, often through the influence of individuals whom we hold dear, or look up to and desire to embody. Tobacco usage had become a prevalent way of life amongst those in our vicinity during our formative years.

From our childhood days, it was innate for us to mirror the way of life of those in our surroundings, much like how both Indigenous children and affluent Jet-set youth instinctively assimilate themselves into their respective environs. However, numerous individuals have expressed to me that their initial impetus was due to the influence of their peers."

Upon careful consideration, I recommend that it was not precisely peer pressure. It was peer adventure.

That is the activity in which us youngsters were engaging. Once more, it can be asserted that the majority of individuals were not coerced by any means or threat of force. We were indulging in a joyful social gathering, relishing the company of our companions, seeking to explore fascinating and daring experiences, and yearning to mature and develop. For a brief moment, we were inclined to experiment with the lifestyle typically attributed to socially distinguished individuals. Or rebel people. Brave people. Following our initial experimentation with this particular lifestyle, we subsequently engaged in it on multiple occasions. Successively and progressively, as one situation led to another, we gradually assimilated this novel way of living into our own.

I designated my initial literary work concerning smoking cessation as The Enlightened Smoker's Guide to Quitting since the majority of smokers aspire to become a distinct entity, more authentic and fashionable, in short, they yearn for an awakening. We were initially unaware of our quest for enlightenment, a new lifestyle and persona. However, such exploratory behavior is commonplace among children; actively seeking out novel experiences, responding to life and embarking upon new life adventures. The innate drive to expand one's horizons, embrace transformation, and discover new realms of possibility is inherently beneficial.

Subsequently, the approach yielded certain positive outcomes, albeit to a limited extent. Undoubtedly, smoking provided us with an altered sense of identity - one that may have induced a greater sense of authenticity, coolness and maturity, albeit to a modest extent. I had the privilege of embarking upon a remarkable adventure, acquiring insights into this novel way of living. The impact of smoking did not demonstrate significant magnitude. Acquiring knowledge on the smoking lifestyle was a novel and pleasurable experience, and thus, it was accepted. If we had not derived pleasure and enjoyment from that lifestyle, we would not have persisted with it. A significant number of our acquaintances experimented with the habit of smoking, yet they did not derive pleasure from it. Individuals who did not derive pleasure from the aforementioned way of living subsequently relinquished their adherence to such a lifestyle.

Allow me to provide an alternative phrasing in a more formal tone: "It is worth noting that refraining from smoking can be approached as an opportunity to incorporate a delightful new way of life into one's routine."

Despite the lack of usage of such terminology, is it not congruent with our initial behavior upon starting to smoke? When we initially took up smoking, we experienced certain physical effects that were unfamiliar and disorienting, albeit enjoyable - which spurred us on to continue. Similarly, the physical effects of abstaining from smoking may initially seem peculiar and disorienting, but can be just as stimulating if approached with an open mindset. In both instances - adopting and abandoning smoking - it is the prospect of a novel lifestyle that provides a source of motivation to pursue this path.

To reiterate, it is feasible to utilize the same ramp to exit Smoke City that was used to gain entry previously. We ought to permit ourselves to recollect the bravery, amusement, and daring mentality we once possessed as youths when we surreptitiously experimented with a novel way of life, aspiring to be trendy and assimilate.

In our present state of maturity, we have come to realize that refraining from smoking is, in fact, a subtle endeavor to embrace a sophisticated, contemporary, and even enlightened way of life. There exists no age limit to learn and embrace a novel lifestyle, just as in our younger years, we did not harbor the notion of being too young for it.

Allen Carr, acclaimed for his bestselling book "Alan Carr's Easy Way to Quit Smoking", was a smoker of five packs a day. You must exert effort towards the habit of reaching for a smoke before getting out of bed and using the hot tip of the old one to light your new cigarette, in order to quit smoking. Carr attested that he found the process relatively uncomplicated upon his ultimate cessation of smoking. Even though he has authored numerous literary works pertaining to the concept of simplicity and organized a five-hour seminar to outline his philosophy, he essentially condenses the essence of his teachings to a mere two sentences in his books: "

1. Formal tone: "Resolve to abstain from smoking permanently;"

2. Please do not despair over it. Rejoice!

It remains uncertain if Carr apprehended the true magnitude of the potency of his second counsel. I frequently inquire of my clients whether they experienced a period of despondency at the commencement of their smoking habit. Inevitably, their response is typically one of amusement, accompanied by a smile or laughter. No, of course not.

Once more, let us employ the same entry point to quit smoking as the one we utilized to commence. We have the opportunity to derive an equal amount of pleasure and excitement from refraining from smoking temporarily as we once derived from indulging in smoking in the moment. Is it feasible to attain a resolution with such apparent simplicity? May I inquire as to the methodology used to accomplish this task? We can achieve this by refraining from despondency, embracing self-acceptance, and adopting the abstaining from smoking as a pleasurable and novel way of life.

A lifestyle? Once more, the act of smoking is something that is frequently engaged in by us. Abstaining from smoking is an action we discontinue.

It can be observed that individuals frequently adopt lifestyles by abstaining from certain actions. For example:

The vegetarian way of life encompasses the abstinence from consumptions of meat, while some individuals choose to follow a lifestyle devoid of watching television. Some individuals opt to abstain from using foul language, refrain from desiring what belongs to others, avoid consuming alcohol, decline to support the Republican or Democratic parties, or elect to refrain from voting altogether.

Certainly, we can opt for a way of life aligned with our actions, such as engaging in uncommitted sexual encounters or habitual consumption of alcohol (sometimes these two paths coincide!) Alternatively, we can choose to don robes and recite mantras or embark on a daily five-mile jog.

However, the decision to refrain from smoking can be regarded as a conscious lifestyle choice. Indeed, the current lifestyle we uphold is immensely gratifying. It follows that giving up smoking is not motivated by a desire to embrace woe and desolation. (You did not commence smoking with the intention to experience displeasure.) You are now ceasing the act of smoking, and instead, choosing to refrain from this habit for the identical basis that you initially began smoking: due to the desire of having a more enjoyable and fulfilling life. Yes?

May I inquire as to the methodology we should employ to achieve that objective? This matter has already been addressed previously. The fundamental lifestyle practice that I impart to a majority of my clientele is the "Enjoy Life" principle.

The fundamental principle of leading a fulfilling life is defined as the Enjoy Life Lifestyle Principle:

Taking pleasure in our existence is the most salubrious, inherent, and affectionate act we can undertake, not only for ourselves but for those in our proximity.

Finding 1: Our lives are only momentarily enjoyed by us.

Observation 2: Indubitably, we tend to forsake the pleasures of life when indulging deeply into the activities we are engaged in, be it through cogitation, sentiment or action, rather than surrendering ourselves to the present moment.

To enhance the quality of our lives, we adopt the concept of a Lifestyle Practice, wherein we divert the focus from the activity at hand and redirect it towards cherishing the present moment, regardless of the nature of the task.

We consistently engage in this uncomplicated exercise of finding pleasure in the present moment - regardless of the cognitions, sentiments, perceptions, or conducts that may arise during such moments. We conform to this way of life simply by relishing being present in the present moment whenever we recollect it, regardless of wherever we might find ourselves. [1]

Ah, once again we find ourselves at Walmart.

This represents the adaptation of our way of living. Our current objective is to enhance our ability to relish life's simple pleasures, one moment at a time, even in the midst of unfavorable circumstances or activities. The quality of our lives is not determined by the nature of our activities. The outcome is not contingent upon our thoughts. It is not contingent upon our subjective emotions. It is contingent upon shifting the focus away from actions and redirecting it to one's presence in the current moment. Henceforth, this lifestyle remains accessible to anyone regardless of their current situation.

Upon careful examination, isn't this "lifestyle practice" precisely what we are attempting to accomplish with our smoking habits, albeit with limited success? During the act of briefly stopping to smoke, are we not attempting to enhance our quality of life, however momentarily and regardless of any concurrent activities? Do we not tend to overlook smoking during times of contentment when we are thoroughly engrossed in relishing our lives?

Once again, the uncomplicated yet pleasurable way of living that we are assimilating, is not founded upon obligatory actions, previous deeds, or anticipated accomplishments. Therefore, the non-smoking lifestyle is inherently less complicated, requiring less effort and presenting a more refined way of living when compared to the smoking lifestyle, which necessitates constant activity, preparation, and corrective action. On the contrary, such a novel way of life is firmly founded on the sheer appreciation of existence, at present, irrespective of our thoughts, emotions, perceptions, or conduct.

Should it come to your recollection or observation, it is quite evident that this is a common behavior exhibited by children. The majority of children tend to derive pleasure from their daily activities on a consistent basis. They are presently savoring the gift of existence, until we impart upon them the need to prioritize action, until we assert the importance of action.

When we grant ourselves the authorization to acquire this novel way of life i.e. diverting the stress from constant action and focusing on the present moment instead, we experience the essence of innate liberty. We come to a realization that we can derive pleasure in our authentic selves, irrespective of the thoughts, emotions or physical sensations that surface within us at any given instant. Through the practice of contentment in the present moment, even for brief intervals during the day, we come to realize that erstwhile propensities, patterns and compulsions hold lesser sway or impel us less. We are not actively engaged in conflict with them, yet we are not influenced by their actions either. Focusing on existence rather than actions is the gateway to liberation.

It appears to be a relatively uncomplicated concept, does it not? By enabling ourselves to fully embrace the present moment, it becomes possible for us to relinquish smoking and move forward. Our education and societal upbringing instill the belief that we must take proactive steps to overcome our smoking addiction, in the same way that we are conditioned to diligently pursue means of finding fulfillment in our daily lives. I have discerned, as my esteemed clients have, that this training is deficient in quality. We may find pleasure in our existence at any given instant, irrespective of our actions, provided that we grant ourselves the opportunity to experience such contentment.

Regarding smoking cessation, are there any recommended actions for us to undertake upon discontinuing our smoking habit? I am afraid that there is no obligation for us to undertake any action. We derive pleasure from the present instance, disregarding any thoughts, emotions or physical experiences that may arise and dissipate. We cease fighting ourselves. To clarify, our present approach involves embracing a distinct form of acceptance regarding our current experiences. We enjoy a life unencumbered by the tumults of conflict and strife. Ahh...

Okay. Everyone please board the bus. Enjoy whatever reactions you might be having to this chapter. If you are inclined to do so, you may employ the "change of lifestyle" strategy to avail yourself of the opportunity to make use of the Easy Exit Off Ramp, thereby exiting from the current situation.

Regrettably, we must inform you that Smoke City no longer offers tobacco products. You already know everything you need to know. However, there is no expectation or obligation in this situation. It is not incumbent upon you to undertake the responsibility of Taking the Off Ramp. We are currently embarked on an exciting and hopefully fruitful expedition.

Let us proceed with driving the bus along the old vicinity, in an endeavor to locate the youth who once sought a ride and we had the privilege to encounter many years prior. Let us relish this present moment and fully embrace the journey that lies ahead, the unfolding expedition on this magnificent planet.

Stomach Relaxing

The technique of diaphragmatic breathing focuses specifically on strengthening the abdominal muscles, thereby facilitating an individual's ability to achieve complete respiration.

To do the activity:

• Place one's hand or a small object gently on the abdominal region.

7

Slowly inhale through the nostrils while observing the degree to which the stomach expands.

Exhale through the oral cavity.

• Inhale through the nostrils, focusing on elevating the stomach higher than the preceding breath.

Exhale deeply and strive to lengthen each exhalation to surpass the duration of each inhalation, with each repetition.

At periodic intervals, it is advisable to perform shoulder rolls in both forward and backward directions, and to gently turn one's head from side to side in order to ensure that the exercise routine does not contribute to any excessive chest pressure.

8

To enhance pulmonary function, it is recommended to practice diaphragmatic breathing and pursed lip breathing techniques for approximately 5 to 10 minutes.

minutes consistently.

9

10

Chapter 3

Stretch Preparing

If one happens to experience fatigue or exhaustion during exercise, it is highly recommended to resort to interval training as a more viable alternative to continuous exercise.

The process of preparing for an endurance activity entails alternating between short periods of vigorous and less demanding physical exertions. For example, an individual may attempt to walk at an elevated pace for a duration of one minute, succeeded by walking at a more moderate speed for a duration of two minutes, in a repeated sequence.

11

In addition, an individual may engage in a strength training regimen lasting for a minute, such as bicep curls or squats, followed by a leisurely walk for a duration of 2-3 minutes.

Engaging in stretching exercises allows for the lungs to undergo a recuperative period before being subjected to further evaluation.

Whenever an activity triggers a state of heightened mental activation, it is advisable to step back momentarily. It can facilitate the practice of pursed-lip breathing to manage breathing difficulties until the agitation subsides.

Benefits Of Smoking Cessation On Health

After a brief cessation period, the majority of individuals tend to observe the benefits of abstaining from smoking. As the critical organs of the lungs and heart commence a process of self-restoration, the overall state of well-being continues to improve. A number of these modifications are set to occur within a consistent timeframe, albeit the resulting effects may vary from individual to individual. Cessation of smoking is likely to yield a diverse range of advantageous outcomes for the physical well-being of an individual.

1). Improvement of Cardiovascular Functioning

The nicotine present in tobacco induces the emission of several substances including carbon monoxide, which escalates blood pressure and accelerates heart rate. Similar results are achieved through the utilization of e-cigarette fluids containing nicotine for vaping. As soon as you inhale, the impact commences.

Upon abstaining from smoking, an individual can observe a notable amelioration in their cardiac rate, blood pressure, and bloodstream within the initial 24-hour period. Following the cessation of your last cigarette or vape session, the likelihood of experiencing a myocardial infarction shall begin to decrease in a matter of hours.

Heart disease is the foremost cause of mortality within the United States and frequently results in fatalities amongst smokers. Abstaining from smoking permanently can result in a significant 50% reduction in the likelihood of experiencing a heart attack.

All individuals who choose to cease smoking are expected to observe a significant enhancement in their cardiovascular health parameters. Nevertheless, variation in an individual's predisposition to hypertension and heart disease necessitates that the definition of 'normal' may fluctuate.

2). Heightened gustatory and olfactory sensations leading to intensified flavors.

The majority of individuals will experience a noticeable improvement in their olfactory and gustatory senses within 48 hours of ceasing exposure, with progressive enhancement over the subsequent weeks.

The influence of cigarettes on the gustatory and olfactory senses results in the direct impairment of these faculties.

The amalgamation of nicotine and other components present in tobacco smoke, when exposed to warm air, has the tendency to impair taste receptors and diminish vascularity that aids in nerve stimulations. The olfactory capacity is impeded by the analogous vascular constriction that occurs within the nasal cavity. Upon cessation of smoking, one may develop an enhanced appreciation for flavors and aromas.

3). Diminished indications of withdrawal

When individuals make the decision to cease smoking, they oftentimes experience concerns pertaining to the onset of cravings and withdrawal symptoms associated with nicotine. Generally, the presence of nicotine within the body will dissipate entirely within a span of three days following the cessation of the aforementioned habit. The cessation of smoking will entail a succession of withdrawal symptoms, including but not limited to severe headaches, heightened tension, insatiable cravings, extreme irritability, sleeplessness, and fatigue.

Appetitive urges may be effectively mitigated through the implementation of alternative activities, such as engaging in exercise or walking, until such a time that the desire for consumption subsides.

Within a month of cessation, the nicotine-sensitive receptors in your brain will begin to normalize their functionality. Over a period of several weeks to a month, on average, your nervous system will gradually adapt to the absence of nicotine resulting in improvement of the most severe debilitating symptoms that you are experiencing.

4). Managing Cravings

Subsequently, the focus shifts towards comprehending and reforming the psychological motivations that prompt smoking behavior. The aforementioned behaviors encompass the inclination to engage in tobacco smoking (or e-cigarette use) for the purpose of relaxation, appetite suppression, socialization, or culminating a gratifying meal.

Persistent behavioral cravings may endure for several months, notwithstanding the complete elimination of nicotine from one's system. When these habits are deeply ingrained psychological patterns that have developed over a period spanning several years or even decades, they could be erroneously identified as symptoms of withdrawal.

As soon as your desires manifest, it is recommended to observe the aspects that may have eluded your comprehension. They will aid you in identifying the underlying causes of these cravings, enabling you to formulate and implement a plan to circumvent them.

As an illustration, in case tension prompts an urge for smoking, delve into mind-body therapies as a means to mitigate and alleviate your stress. If smoking is perceived as a communal activity, consider exploring alternative and wholesome means of social engagement with associates, such as taking a stroll or increasing the duration of social interaction.

Whilst the pangs of nicotine may present a formidable challenge, they usually dissipate within the initial few weeks of abstinence. Nicotine replacement therapy (NRT) has the potential to mitigate nicotine cravings and withdrawal manifestations. Various approaches, such as engaging in recreational activities and implementing stress-alleviation techniques, may also prove advantageous.

An elevation in the circulation of blood.

After a span of one to three months of refraining from smoking, there will be a substantial enhancement in the circulation of blood.

The potent vasoconstrictive effects of nicotine give rise to the constriction of blood arteries. Virtually every bodily organ system is affected by this. The proficient functioning of the body's internal organs is impeded in the absence of efficient transportation of oxygen and nutrients, and elimination of carbon dioxide and toxins from tissues is hindered through the process of blood circulation.

Improved skin tone, increased elasticity and heightened ability to retain moisture are all positive outcomes of augmented blood flow. The complete reversal of skin damage (exemplified by the emergence of spider veins in the face and legs) is not guaranteed by smoking cessation. Nonetheless, after a span of several months, a remarkable distinction is generally evident.

6). Enhanced Fertility

The act of smoking can have detrimental effects on the capacity of a female to conceive. It has the potential to compromise the ability to conceive and heighten the likelihood of experiencing miscarriage and preterm delivery. As per a study conducted in the year 2017, indulging in smoking six or more cigarettes in a day has an adverse impact on the fertility of the female population. Over the course of a three-month abstinence period, there is a likelihood of heightened fertility. The cessation of smoking often results in an increase in conception rates in the span of a year, although empirical evidence implies that smoking might have a long-standing deleterious impact on fertility.

7). Improved Lung Function

After discontinuing smoking, the lungs commence a reparative process. Dyspnea is among the symptoms that ameliorate through the gradual elimination of carbon monoxide from the circulatory system. Tobacco inhalation exacerbates airway lining irritation. Nevertheless, smoking cessation averts the inhalation of harmful toxins, consequently enabling the airways' recuperation process to commence.

Cilia, the diminutive hair-like projections present on the surface of lung cells involved in capturing bacteria and mucus, distributing them toward the back of the throat for swallowing, are observed to resume their functionality upon cessation of the habit. This fosters the clearance of the respiratory system and facilitates the body's elimination of accumulated mucus.

Upon ceasing smoking, an improvement in lung function and enhanced circulation are expected to occur within the initial month. After the completion of nine months, the cilia commence their regular functioning and indications such as coughing and respiratory distress diminish in incidence. The chances of developing bladder, kidney, lung, mouth, and throat cancer are significantly decreased within a decade of smoking cessation, thereby underscoring the advantageous impact of long-term smoking abstinence on an individual's health.

However, smoking exerts unfavorable impacts on one's health, some of which endure even after its cessation. As an example, emphysema, a medical condition characterized by inflammation, constriction, and swelling of the airways, has the potential to cause enduring changes to the air passages which may result in lasting impairment of lung function.

8) Enduring Benefits of Smoking Cessation in the Long Run

Abstaining from smoking will likely result in substantial long-term improvements in your health and overall welfare, while also granting you a number of immediate physiological advantages.

After a span of one to two years post quitting, there is a considerable decline in the likelihood of developing coronary heart disease. Subsequently, over the upcoming years, this probability diminishes with a consistent pace. In a period of three to six years, the probability of your susceptibility to coronary heart disease shall diminish by approximately 50%, compared to the likelihood when you were a smoking individual.

Over time, the probability of passing away due to stroke is likely to approximate that of an individual who has never indulged in smoking. Furthermore, abstaining from smoking reduces your probability of developing cancer in the long run. Within a decade of cessation, the probability of acquiring malignancies affecting the oral cavity, oropharynx, and larynx is diminished by 50%. The probability of developing lung cancer is reduced by 50% during the ten to fifteen years subsequent to smoking cessation.

9). Enhance the Probability of Successful Cessation.

It is imperative to ensure adequate preparedness prior to embarking on a smoking cessation regimen. This facilitates the formulation of strategies essential for the elimination of transient symptoms. Furthermore, it alleviates the strain caused by unresolved ambiguity. On occasion, the cessation and recuperation procedure can prove more distressing than apprehension towards what is yet to come.

Regardless of the approach you undertake, it is imperative that you do not embark on it in isolation. To avail support from your acquaintances, it is advisable to communicate your expectations to your friends and family members. Collaborate with your healthcare provider to determine the most suitable smoking cessation interventions prior to onset of symptoms, such as counseling and group therapy, instead of hastily seeking solutions upon manifestation of symptoms.

Ceasing smoking not only yields immediate health benefits, but also garners enduring advantages that can persist for years, if not decades. As per the Centers for Disease Control and Prevention (CDC), quitting smoking may lead to an increase of up to a decade in one's life expectancy.

The act of quitting smoking yields numerous health benefits, which tend to escalate with the duration of one's sustained abstinence. Individuals may also find pleasure in the opportunity to engage in social interactions while smoking indoors, and experience a reduction in respiratory distress during routine activities.

Furthermore, cessation of tobacco use has the potential to avert its adverse impact on your physical appearance, encompassing skin aging, dental decay, and periodontal disease.

Strategies for Managing Nicotine Cravings during Smoking Cessation Utilizing the 5 Ds.

The bundle of strategies known as the five Ds can aid in promptly curbing the urge to engage in smoking. Cessation of smoking results in the manifestation of nicotine withdrawal symptoms in the body, which poses a considerable challenge to individuals aiming to quit the habit.

Negative affect, unpleasant physical sensations, and persistent urges to smoke can ensue as a consequence of cessation. Nevertheless, even subsequent to the withdrawal phase, the lingering desire to smoke may persist for several months.

The quartet of Ds represents effective coping techniques that may be utilized independently or in conjunction to regulate one's urges, irrespective of one's progress towards overcoming the addiction.

Four elements can be categorized as the Ds:

1). Delay\sDistract

2). Drink water

3). Deep inhalation

4). Engage in a constructive discourse on intentionally postponing smoking until the urge to smoke has diminished. Despite their inherent challenge, cravings tend to dissipate rather expeditiously.

Delay

Please refrain from smoking until the urge has dissipated. Despite being unpleasant, cravings usually subside expeditiously.

It may come as a surprise to discover that the urge dissipates within a mere ten-minute period. If the issue persists, kindly allow a brief period of approximately 10 minutes to elapse before attempting again. During the interim, you are welcome to engage in several of the four Ds. You have the liberty to defer any number of times throughout the course of each day.

Drink Water

The consumption of water is potentially efficacious in lower craving levels. Moreover, adequate consumption of water may alleviate certain withdrawal symptoms associated with smoking cessation including cravings, fatigue, migraines, and perspiration.

During smoking cessation, a prior smoker may experience orofacial discomfort due to cravings for cigarettes.

Consuming a single serving of water may induce a sensation of satiety. An alternative course of action would be to consume a toothpick, sugar-free gum, or mints, which not only offer a pleasant taste but also have the possibility of minimizing some of your cravings.

Deep Inhalation

If you experience an urge to smoke, attempt practicing deep breathing maneuvers. Employing prolonged and profound abdominal respiration can assist in relinquishing notions pertaining to smoking and enhancing one's capacity to concentrate. They have the potential to foster a serene state of being in both your physical and mental faculties.

Search for a tranquil location in which you may settle. Inhale profoundly and permit the air to occupy your lower abdominal region. Exhale gradually through either your mouth or nostrils.

Kindly ensure that you maintain a composed and comfortable state upon one's repetition of this exercise several times. One may try out a diverse range of deep breathing techniques. Endeavor to diligently practice for a minimum of 10 minutes each day or whenever the urge to smoke arises.

As per a study, engaging in the practice of yoga can be beneficial in cessation of smoking.

Furthermore, the adverse ramifications arising from the cessation of nicotine consumption. Such conduct fosters an enduring level of well-being and nurtures individuals to value themselves and their physical selves.

Finally, it is a challenging task to quit smoking, and it can be quite vexing to have persistent cravings for cigarettes. Please be reminded that it is within your discretion to devise a distinctive approach in managing these impulses. The proposed approach entails the incorporation of the aforementioned four Ds.

Upon the emergence of any craving, it is advisable to experiment with various options to ascertain those which align with your preferences and needs the most effectively. In order to sustain one's determination during times of struggle, it is recommended to seek support from either a trustworthy friend or a reliable support group. With the abstention from nicotine, the urges will progressively diminish and ameliorate through dedicated effort.

Discuss

Kindly apprise an individual who possesses knowledge of your preferences regarding your cravings. It is imperative to bear in mind that you are not alone, regardless of whether you feel inclined to smoke. There exists a multitude of additional support groups that individuals may access to aid them in their efforts to quit smoking.

If you are experiencing any cravings, we suggest that you explore the option of reaching out to a recovery group, seeking the company of a motivating neighbor, or seeking the support of a family member who is empathetic and understanding.

Individuals may derive motivation to refrain from succumbing to their smoking urges through the companionship of a cessation partner or the emotional bolstering of a support system. They can aid you in maintaining accountability towards your goal of abstinence from smoking.

Requesting another individual to aid in reminding you of the motives behind your decision to abstain at times of fleeting desires can serve to enhance your ability to regulate impulses.

Upon the next occasion when you experience the inclination to engage in smoking, it is recommended that you delay such action by a duration of 10 minutes.

Please make note of your emotions and thoughts as the clock approaches its completion. Does the inclination to engage in smoking persist?

It may come as a surprise to discover that the urge dissipates within a span of 10 minutes. Should the issue persist, it is advisable to wait for an additional 10 minutes. During the interim period, you are at liberty to engage in any of the remaining four tasks of relevance. You are allowed to defer the activity as per your convenience and as many times as deemed essential during the entire day.

Direct one's focus away from thoughts of smoking by engaging in alternative activities. Regular physical activity may facilitate an increase in vitality and serve as a distraction from urges to indulge in cravings.

Engage in some physical activity such as traversing your home's stairway multiple times or engaging in a jog around the vicinity.

2). Introducing alterations to one's daily regimen may foster the ability to conquer urges. Suspend your present undertaking and initiate a new task. I would suggest attempting to solve a crossword puzzle as an alternative to viewing television. If it is anticipated that smoking will not be allowed, kindly contemplate arranging a trip to a civic library, museum or theater.

3.) Divest oneself of the impulses of smoking by engaging in alternative activities. Engaging in fitness activities can potentially enhance your energy levels and provide a constructive diversion from indulging in cravings.

Consider traversing your staircase multiple times or engaging in a brief jog around the neighborhood.

Implementing alterations to one's dietary intake may assist with surmounting cravings, whilst interrupting ongoing activities and initiating novel pursuits. Consider engaging in the activity of solving a jigsaw puzzle as a viable alternative to watching television. If it is anticipated that tobacco usage will not be allowed, it is advisable to contemplate arranging a trip to a civic library, museum, or theatre.

Utilize All The Available Assistance At Your Disposal.

Let Others Help You

As previously mentioned, achieving smoking cessation solely through personal efforts is a challenging task. Ensure that you avail yourself of all available forms of support from individuals in your surroundings. There are abundant methods available to accomplish this task. As an illustration, it is possible to apprise your familial, social, and professional circle of your determined resolution to relinquish smoking, and solicit their valuable backing. Research indicates that the probability of achieving success in smoking cessation is significantly enhanced through the assistance of additional support.

Enrollment in telephone, group, or individual counseling programs may be considered. Engaging in counseling services has the potential to significantly enhance one's likelihood of achieving success. This approach can further assist you in recognizing and surmounting circumstances that may provoke the inclination to smoke a cigarette. At present, there exist costless software applications that can be found at nearby healthcare establishments and medical centers. You can contact the health department within your locality to obtain relevant information on the various programs being offered in your vicinity. If you are a resident of the United States, there is also a complimentary telephonic counseling service available.

It is also recommended that individuals schedule appointments with their healthcare providers, such as doctors, dentists, pharmacists, nurses, psychologists, or smoking cessation counselors or coaches, particularly if they are considering utilizing medications.

One may also consider integrating cessation counseling with the utilization of either prescription or over-the-counter medication. The amalgamation of these two methods has demonstrated significantly improved outcomes as compared to employing either of them singularly.

Acquiring the aid of individuals in close proximity to you is crucial, for their absence would inevitably impede your conquest in this endeavor. With their assistance, the challenges at hand will be mitigated, reducing the level of difficulty to a more manageable extent.

Phytotherapeutic And Naturopathic Solutions For Smoking Cessation

Given the costliness of prescription medication designated to assist smokers in their effort to attain cessation, there has been a marked rise in the prevalence of utilization of herbal substitutes. It is feasible for one to easily obtain and cultivate herbs within the confines of their own backyard. Moreover, conventional medicines often contain synthetic or hazardous compounds that may trigger adverse reactions, whereas herbs are predominantly organic and impart beneficial outcomes. Presented herein are the foremost three herbal interventions that may serve as efficacious aids for individuals seeking to cease their smoking habit.

Herbal Remedy #1: LOBELIA

Scientific research has demonstrated the effectiveness of this herb in mitigating the symptoms associated with nicotine withdrawal during the initial weeks following smoking cessation. Despite its potential benefits, it is critical to exercise caution and consume this substance in minute quantities due to its high level of toxicity.

Herbal Remedy #2: GINGER

The herb serves as an inherent purifying agent that expels nicotine from the system by inducing perspiration. It is claimed that this substance may assist smokers in managing specific nicotine withdrawal symptoms, including but not limited to anxiety and nausea.

Herbal Remedy #3: ST. JOHN'S WORT

The herb has properties that help in overcoming anxiety, depression, imbalanced appetites, and other nicotine withdrawal symptoms that occur during the first weeks.

Regarding potential homeopathic interventions for smoking cessation, two highly-recommended options include the consumption of alkaline foods and the utilization of aromatherapy. Consumption of alkaline-rich foods like almonds, porridge, raisins, spinach, and various greens has been observed to reduce the frequency of cravings, which, in turn, acts as a deterrent to smoking. The olfactory sensation emitted by various oils, including but not limited to lemon, lavender, and orange, evidences an inhibitory effect on cravings and ameliorates specific symptoms arising from nicotine withdrawal. This approach entails the application of a mixture of oil and water via spraying in specific zones of the dwelling, thereby inducing a calming ambiance that can aid individuals in addressing their struggle with nicotine dependence.

In addition, various herbal and homeopathic remedies for individuals who smoke entail:

- SALT. Ingesting small amounts a day to reduce cravings.

- **OAT STRAW.** In the form of tea, it has the potential to promptly alleviate anxiety.

- **VALERIAN.** Assists in the management of sleeping disorders that arise due to the cessation of nicotine consumption.

- **CAYENNE PEPPER.** Added to meals to reduce cravings.

HONEY. Administered in recommended smaller amounts daily to mitigate yearning and surmount indications of nicotine abstinence.

A Simple and Efficient Four-Step Program for Smoking Cessation.

Given the multitude of cessation choices available, certain individuals who smoke encounter difficulties and occasional perplexity in commencing their quitting journey, unsure of which strategies and regimens to adopt. The pivotal aspect towards ultimately and effectively ceasing the habit of smoking is to devise a methodical strategy that encompasses a sequence of actions to adhere to. Simultaneously undertaking multiple tasks fails to be an efficacious strategy for accomplishing any objective. Achieving the intended results necessitates methodically advancing through each stage of the process.

The optimal strategy for smoking cessation must be facile and comprehensible. It doesn't need to have a huge number of steps, this would be too complicated and difficult to pursue.

An ideal strategy should be designed to promote progress by imposing simple, efficient procedures instead of deterring advancement through intricate, time-consuming phases. Foremost among all, it is imperative that a smoking cessation plan is efficacious.

The comprehensive method for smokers to ultimately cease smoking entails four effortless and methodical steps that guarantee the best results. These are:

Step one involves acknowledging the true extent of one's smoking habit.

The initial course of action for smokers should involve disclosing the quantity of cigarettes consumed on a daily basis and the duration of their reliance on smoking. The act of admission is accompanied by acceptance, which subsequently paves the way for transformation and enhancement. It is highly recommended to identify the underlying reasons for the smoking habit during this stage.

Secondly, PREPARING FOR THE DAY OF CESSATION FROM SMOKING.

Smokers may not necessarily be required to engage in an immediate cessation of smoking. The process of transitioning from a smoker to a non-smoker with success entails a gradual journey in which an individual must first conscientiously persuade themselves of their personal necessity, desire, and obligation to cease smoking. For the successful completion of Day 1, it is imperative for one to exhibit full-fledged dedication and absolute assurance in advance, so as to prevent any obstacles in the course of quitting, which can compel an individual to recommence the entire process anew. During this phase, it is crucial to compile a comprehensive enumeration of the grounds that motivate an individual to renounce smoking, encompassing both personal and health-related factors.

Proceeding to the third step, which involves the identification of personalized strategies tailored to effectively facilitate cessation.

It is imperative for individuals with smoking addiction to carefully assess the compatibility of various techniques and treatments with their schedule, financial resources, and daily routine, in order to determine the most suitable approach towards overcoming their habit. The therapeutic approaches may vary, encompassing attendance to psychotherapeutic sessions for multiple days in a week, involvement in self-help communities, practicing mindfulness exercises, resorting to pharmacological substances, and employing nicotine replacements. Individuals who engage in tobacco use may also seek the professional guidance of medical practitioners and experts to deliberate upon the most suitable course of treatment for their condition.

Phase four entails the SUSTAINMENT OF A SMOKE-FREE LIFESTYLE.

The ultimate stage is achieved following several months or even years of therapy, and necessitates a significant amount of endurance and determination. Intermittent urges may arise, however, the key to maintaining a smoke-free existence entails employing positive reinforcement, mindfulness, and rejuvenation. Self-recompense may be observed upon achieving significant milestones in one's journey towards overcoming a habit, for instance, successfully abstaining from smoking for a year or surmounting a challenging urge. When occasional cravings arise, one may engage in the practice of recalling the underlying motivations for their initial decision to abstain and the anticipated benefits thereof as a means of reinforcing their commitment. One may engage in renewal by seeking alternative means of diverting their focus from smoking, such as exploring new hobbies or interests.

Manage And Regulate Your Emotions.

It is of utmost significance for us to acknowledge and comprehend the emotions and the emotional associations we establish with cigarettes in our psyche; such an endeavor can yield remarkable outcomes.

The difficulty we face is that we are often controlled by our emotions whether positive or negative, so we have no clear direction in our life, as a boat in the middle of the rough sea.

To elucidate the issue at hand, consider the following example: in the event of experiencing anger due to certain compelling circumstances, this unfavorable emotion tends to overpower us and results in uttering and committing actions that we would later remorse and would never have sought to undertake. Ultimately, this might cause us sorrow and necessitate making amends with an undeserving party.

It is imperative for us to express this emotion, as suppressing it would only result in its internalization. This alternative can prove to be disadvantageous as it involves the accumulation of adverse energy within us, which may cause an adverse impact on our physical, psychological, and emotional well-being. Consequently, our day or even an entire week could be ruined. Consequently, it is imperative that we consistently transform any unfavorable emotional energy into a constructive force.

Henceforth, it is imperative to address our emotions that foster a profound connection with our innermost self and emotional facet that tend to overpower our logical reasoning. It represents a formidable source of energy.

It is highly consequential to leverage such tools for our personal benefit, as they hold the potential to initiate a transformative shift in our lives.

Emotions give rise to affective bonds that can have both positive or negative connotations, as exemplified by the instance of cigarette usage. Immediate measure must be taken to sever any negative connections that may be detrimental to our interests.

To undertake the examination of emotions, the ensuing process encompasses the subsequent phases: firstly, identify the fundamental emotions that are associated with smoking. For instance, postulating that the act of smoking fosters one's sense of self-assurance signifies that you have established a cognitive connection between the act of smoking and the emotional experience of feeling confident.

2) Sever the association between affectivity and the process of smoking.

Concede to yourself that cigarettes do not offer a viable solution to bolstering your self-esteem. Rather, they serve as a deceptive and transitory measure to address your perceived needs. In other words, smoking will not promote self-confidence in your daily life. Consider the possibility that there may have been instances in which you experienced notable self-assurance, yet abstained from smoking, as well as moments during which you engaged in smoking, yet did not experience a corresponding sense of self-confidence. The presence of smoke can be misleading with regards to one's level of self-assurance.

3) Foster a novel alliance at an emotional level. Reflect upon the instances wherein you experienced self-assurance and abstained from smoking. Ponder upon a matter that you are extremely certain about and recognize the augmented self-assurance that it has brought about. Foster the belief that this sensation can be sustained and maintained in the forthcoming days and weeks. Envision a future where you portray unwavering confidence in yourself. Reiterate to yourself continuously: "I am certain of my desire to exclusively inhale pure air" and "Each instance of inhaling pure air bolsters my self-assurance."

By means of this procedure, we sever the earlier unfavorable emotional association and establish a fresh constructive emotional linkage.

Cigarettes can elicit a plethora of emotions and foster deep emotional connections. An instance of such behavior could involve the act of smoking for the following purposes:

- Feel Self-confident

- Feel Stronger

- Overcoming Shyness

- Try Pleasure

- Try Joy

- Overcome Fear

- Create Sharing

- Feel Love

- Overcome Stress

- Overcome Frustration

- Overcome Anger

- Overcome Boredom

Think and think only that smoking has absolutely nothing to do, with all these emotions! Even those who do not smoke feel this emotion. You can effectively overcome adverse emotions or experience positive ones without resorting to smoking.

When partaking in smoking, it is necessary to discern the emotions that are closely linked to the smoking habit, and which frequently require consideration, subsequently disconnecting said emotions from the habit of smoking. It is imperative that you commence your efforts towards developing better emotional regulation mechanisms in order to guarantee a superior standard of life, thereby enhancing your subjective experience.

Given our understanding of the mechanisms underlying emotional attachments to smoking, it behooves us to consider the impetus for change: whether it is driven by intrinsic motivations or extrinsic pressures. Who, precisely, is the intended beneficiary of such an alteration?

CHAPTER SEVEN

The benefits of cessation

Although the measurements are concerning, it is fortunate that cessation of smoking reduces the likelihood of disease and mortality significantly. The hazards decrease progressively as an individual refrains from tobacco use for a prolonged period.

In point of fact, certain studies suggest that cessation prior to the age of 40 substantially reduces the risk of mortality from smoking-related ailments by approximately 90%.

The aforementioned metrics delineate the health benefits of smoking cessation.

Adverse cardiovascular effects: Following cessation of cigarette smoking for a period of one year, the likelihood of experiencing respiratory failure is significantly reduced.

The risk of suffering a stroke is significantly reduced to a fraction of that of a non-smoker within a period of 2-5 years.

The risk of developing malignant growths, specifically mouth, throat, throat, and bladder cancer, is observed to decrease by approximately 50% within a span of 5 years after cessation, whereas a 10-year cessation period is required for a similar reduction in the incidence of lung cancer.

Shortly after quitting, individuals can experience the following health benefits that can greatly enhance their quality of life and serve as testament to the health benefits of cessation: "

breathing becomes simpler

The consistent and recurrent episodes of hacking and wheezing gradually diminish, eventually ceasing altogether.

The senses of taste and smell exhibit enhancement.

The act of exercising and the respective activities involved therein become progressively simplified.

dissemination to the hands and feet moves along

Although the cessation process may entail certain discomfort, it is often observed that individuals tend to experience a substantial reduction in their daily stress levels within the duration of six months or thereabout, as compared to the time when they were actively smoking.

Cessation of smoking is a personalized journey, whereby the approach that proves efficacious for one individual may not necessarily yield the same outcome for another. Assess one or two techniques in order to determine their optimal performance.

During the process of smoking cessation, the following guidelines may prove to be beneficial:

Prepare a sound rationale for the benefits and wisdom of cessation. Examine these materials at your leisure in the event of an urge to smoke.

Make use of a software application to monitor your progress. Attaining accomplishments such as a tobacco-free day can aid an individual in advancing forward. A plethora of free and paid applications is at one's disposal.

Attempt nicotine substitution items. Nicotine patches, gums, and tablets can assist with lessening desires, making it simpler to oppose at a specific second.

Numerous individuals ascertain that establishing a connection with a healthcare provider for assistance can facilitate permanent cessation of the habit. A medical professional has the authority to prescribe medication such as varenicline (Chantix). Presently, experts recommend this intervention as the primary treatment modality for individuals seeking to quit smoking.

Smoking Is A Habit

A habit denotes a recurrent practice that is frequently performed almost unconsciously. The act of smoking cigarettes has become a customary practice among a significant number of individuals. They may not engage in introspection regarding the reasons behind their smoking habits; rather, it has habituated into their daily routine.

There exist a multitude of factors that could potentially contribute to the formation of a smoking addiction in an individual. Certain individuals may initiate the habit of smoking as a means of conforming to their social circle or cultivating a certain image. Others start because they think it will help them relax or deal with stress. Furthermore, individuals may initiate smoking due to the influence of their social circle, as they have been informed that it is beneficial for their well-being.

For whatever cause, once an individual initiates smoking, discontinuing the habit can pose great difficulty. The addictive nature of nicotine present in cigarettes poses a significant challenge to individuals attempting to quit their use. Despite the formidable challenge of quitting smoking, undertaking the effort to overcome this addiction is unquestionably worthwhile.

How Much Money Does This Habit Cost You

As per the estimations of the U.S. Centers for Disease Control and Prevention, a considerable number of adult smokers in the United States allocate an amount exceeding $100 per month towards their expenditure on cigarettes and tobacco products.

Frequently, individuals expend an amount less than $20 monthly on tobacco products. It is a common perception among smokers that each pack of cigarettes they buy will suffice for a span of three to four days.

Several tobacco products have a price exceeding $100. A considerable proportion of smokers regularly allocate a substantial sum of money to procure tobacco-based commodities each month, yet their expenditure is usually dispersed across a multitude of tobacco products.

It is estimated that the mean expenditure of a typical adult smoker ranges from $2.35 to $3.60 per day towards the purchase of tobacco products. When individuals opt for diverse tobacco products, they may incur an average daily expenditure of $2.95 on smokeless tobacco products and $2.50 on cigars.

For instance, an individual who consumes two packs of cigarettes per day would typically expend approximately $120 on their smoking habit each month.

Several succinct statistics gleaned from a recent survey may prove to be unexpectedly insightful. The mean yearly expenditure incurred by smoking cigarettes, which leads to nicotine dependency, amounts to $11,000. According to certain studies, it has been revealed that the expenses involved can be as much as $15,000.

The remuneration an adult smoker pays for a pack of cigarettes amounts to $7.50. In 2010, an average adult smoker incurred an expenditure of $1.49 for a solitary cigarette. The current price of a pack of cigarettes is nearly quadruple the amount it was in 1970.

According to the World Health Organization, tobacco usage is prevalent among 2 billion individuals globally, whereas 400 million individuals residing in the United States exhibit tobacco consumption. An excess of 80,000 individuals pass away annually as a direct result of tobacco consumption.

Based on current projections, it is anticipated that the global population will experience in excess of 4.8 billion fatalities associated with tobacco consumption by the year 2030.

Over the course of nearly four decades, the United States experienced a notable decline in the number of individuals partaking in cigarette smoking. Despite this positive trend, the number of fatalities resulting from cigarette usage remained alarmingly high, with figures exceeding 480,000 by the year 2003, up from approximately 500,000 in previous decades. Subsequent to that time, there has been no substantial modification in the quantity of individuals who habitually consume cigarettes.

It is imperative to adopt a new approach towards spending.

Individuals endeavoring to give up smoking may wish to contemplate embracing a novel approach towards their expenditure. One possible formal alternative could be: "This may entail allocating the funds that would have been expended on tobacco products into a designated savings account, or alternatively, utilizing said resources towards acquiring long-term assets such as exercise apparatus or healthcare coverage." Several smokers may consider refraining from smoking as a pragmatic approach towards ensuring their long-term health and wellness. Through the implementation of prudent financial measures and adoption of healthy lifestyle practices, they can enhance their likelihood of attaining success.

I tend to opt for cigarettes with a lower nicotine content.

The harmfulness of "light" cigarettes is comparable to that of "regular" cigarettes. According to research findings, cigarettes containing lower levels of nicotine have the potential to result in greater harm. How is that possible? Due to the intrinsic presence of nicotine in tobacco and the need for tobacco companies to mitigate its effects, a range of chemical compounds are utilized in the process. The chemicals employed in this procedure possess toxic properties.

The purported light, superlight, and disparate lower nicotine cigarettes are a form of marketing ploy. Tobacco enterprises have come to the realization that individuals tend to perceive light cigarettes as less deleterious, and hence, continue to engage in smoking merely because of the aforementioned perception. They had contemplated quitting but now they have the option to consume cigarettes formulated with healthier constituents. Moreover, it is noteworthy that the nicotine and tar levels in light cigarettes are comparatively lower, however, it is imperative to note that the quantity of numerous hazardous chemicals responsible for causing cancer remains unaffected.

In addition to that, scholars have discovered that individuals who smoke light cigarettes experience a reduction in their nicotine intake, stimulating them to breathe more profoundly, leading to further pulmonary deterioration. Individuals who consume light cigarettes may likely exhibit increased smoking frequency. The absorption of nicotine in each cigarette is decreased, resulting in expedited depletion of nicotine levels in the body.

This concludes the chapter on justifications. There exists an ample supply of alternatives. As evident from our proficiency in devising narratives and justifications, we possess exceptional skills in the art of persuasion. I am not making an assertion that individuals who smoke are inherently dishonest. It is their sincere belief that cigarettes confer upon them such aesthetic benefits. What other justification could they possibly offer for engaging in such a deleterious conduct?

Subsequent chapters will elucidate the reasons behind our tendency to make excuses and explicate how our brains demonstrate remarkable proficiency in reinforcing our beliefs regarding the same. You will observe how your cognitive faculties might be deceiving you.

What Got You Hooked

The initial few cigarettes that you inhaled may have induced significant discomfort. Majority of us retain vivid recollections of those instances when we first tried smoking and pondered upon the rationale behind such an act. I have a recollection of experiencing an illness accompanied by dizziness. The act of smoking the initial cigarette did not afford an enjoyable sensation. The respiratory system was attempting to signal us that tobacco consumption is detrimental to health and that we ought to desist without delay.

Initially, you faced difficulties in cultivating an addiction, whereas presently, you are grappling with relinquishing it. Such is the inherent character of addiction. Subsequently in life, we all feel remorseful for indulging in our initial cigarette. We were afforded the occasion to heed our physiological responses, indicating that smoking is detrimental. We failed to heed and persisted in smoking. Our neurological systems became accustomed to the presence of nicotine, and before we were aware, addiction had taken hold. It is commonly observed that people often fail to recognize their addiction to nicotine until the point where it becomes irreversible. Many individuals typically acknowledge their addiction after making an attempt to cease such behavior.

A prevalent belief among individuals who do not engage in smoking is that individuals who smoke are generally of frail character. They perceive them as individuals who are highly susceptible to the inception of smoking habits, and subsequently lacking in the willpower necessary to withdraw from such addiction.

Within the group of smokers, there exists a diverse array of individuals, ranging from blue-collar laborers to high-ranking executives and accomplished athletes, medical practitioners, academic scholars, legal professionals, and creative artists. There is no correlation between smoking and one's character. Individuals who do not smoke tobacco were fortunate not to have experienced experimenting with it at an inopportune moment. It is probable for them to fall prey to nicotine addiction, just like us. We have unfortunately erred in our judgment. We succumbed to the exigencies of maturing, the demands of conforming to societal norms. To what extent can we hold children and teenagers accountable for experimenting with behaviors they may have been exposed to through the actions of their guardians, educators, or peers? We aspire to emulate the behavior of senior individuals by engaging in similar activities. During that period of youth, smoking was perceived as fashionable. We held the notion that such an experience would bring about a heightened level of maturity and perceived seniority. I take full responsibility for my addiction and do not attribute it to external factors or individuals. Never did. However, during our youthful years, we often engage in various unwise behaviors. Fortuitously, the majority of those alternative substances do not possess the characteristic of being habit-forming. Smoking is. It is uncommon for individuals to initiate smoking after reaching the age of 30. Considering their age, they possess knowledge on the perils and addictive nature of tobacco smoking, therefore, it is probable that they would refrain from engaging in such activity. Adolescents do not hold such a perspective. Upon initial experimentation, we lack knowledge regarding the addictive properties of smoking. Our comprehension of the potency of nicotine addiction is currently incomplete. It is highly improbable that a considerable number of individuals would initiate smoking if they were fully aware of the adverse health consequences that they are likely to encounter in their future lives because of the habit. If we were aware of the arduousness of ceasing smoking.

The onset of a lifelong addiction can be precipitated by a single imprudent decision.

The prevalence of smoking addiction is higher amongst individuals who engage in the activity, with only a minority of smokers being able to abstain without developing addictive tendencies. Whilst a considerable number among us remain immune to the habit of tobacco smoking, there are those individuals who may be predisposed to becoming habitual smokers. Either embracing smoking and succumbing to addiction, or abstaining from smoking altogether, are the alternatives presented. Our organization does not entertain the notion of a middle ground.

The Potential Advantages To One's Health Resulting From The Practice Of Tobacco Consumption.

It is highly recommended to discontinue smoking if you currently engage in the habit. Cessation of a particular action could be arduous. A considerable majority of individuals who discontinue a particular activity have made multiple unsuccessful attempts and failed to achieve lasting success in the past. All preceding efforts to cease a certain activity should be regarded as valuable learning opportunities, rather than instances of inadequacy or defeat.

There exist various compelling justifications to cease tobacco consumption. The utilization of tobacco over a prolonged duration has the potential to substantially enhance the likelihood of numerous severe health complications, as elaborated on in the preceding chapter.

BENEFITS OF QUITTING
When one abstains from smoking, the ensuing benefits can be relished, such as: Your breath, attire, and tresses will emanate a more pleasant fragrance. Your olfactory sense shall be restored. Food will taste better. Over time, there will be a gradual reduction in the yellowish appearance of your fingers and nails. The gradual whitening of your discolored teeth can be expected. Your children will be healthier and less likely to start smoking. Procuring an apartment or a hotel accommodation would be comparatively straightforward and cost-effective. Your prospects of securing employment may be more favorable. Acquaintances are likely to express greater propensity to take a ride in your automobile or visit your abode. Perhaps it may prove relatively more

convenient to secure an appointment. A considerable number of individuals neither engage in nor appreciate proximity to individuals who smoke. You will save money. Individuals who smoke one pack of cigarettes daily would approximately incur an expenditure of $2,000 annually on the purchase of tobacco products.

HEALTH BENEFITS

Several health benefits commence expeditiously. Every smoke-free week, month, and year improves your health even further. After the cessation of smoking, it takes approximately 20 minutes for the blood pressure and heart rate to revert to their usual state. After a lapse of 12 hours of refraining from smoking, the concentration of carbon monoxide in your bloodstream reaches a state of normalcy. Following the cessation of smoking, there is a discernible enhancement in your circulatory system and an increase in pulmonary function which typically occurs within a period of two to three months. During a period of 1 to 9 months following cessation of the medication, there is an alleviation of symptoms such as coughing and breathing difficulties. The respiratory system exhibits improved mucus processing and enhanced lung clearance, thereby mitigating the susceptibility to respiratory infections. Within a period of less than a year subsequent to cessation of smoking, the chances of developing coronary heart disease are reduced to half as that of a smoker who still continues to smoke. The probability of you suffering a heart attack has been considerably mitigated.

Upon cessation of tobacco use for a period of 5 years, the likelihood of developing cancer of the oral cavity, pharynx, esophagus, and bladder is reduced by 50%. The likelihood of developing cervical cancer in individuals who do not smoke. It is possible for the risk of stroke to reduce to the level of a non-smoker within a period of two to five years. Upon cessation of smoking for a decade, the probability of succumbing to lung cancer reduces by 50% in comparison to those who continue to smoke. After abstinence from smoking for a duration of 15 years, the likelihood of developing coronary heart disease equates to that of an individual who has never smoked. Cessation of smoking can yield additional health advantages such as diminished likelihood of the formation of blood clots in lower extremities that may, otherwise, travel to the lungs; decreased risk of suffering from erectile dysfunction; and diminished obstetric complications like preterm labor and delivery, and infants being born with low birth weight.

The occurrence of both miscarriage and cleft lip has been associated with a diminished probability of infertility arising from impaired sperm quality. Improved dental hygiene, gum health, and skin wellness. Residing alongside infants and young children can result in the more manageable control of asthma, a substantial reduction in emergency room visits, as well as fewer occurrences of colds, ear infections, and pneumonia, thus diminishing the risks of Sudden Infant Death Syndrome (SIDS).

Day 23

Exercise:

Clean something slowly. Kindly allocate an adequate amount of time for the cleaning endeavor, avoiding haste and ensuring comprehensive completion. It is possible for you to tidy up various aspects of your living space, including but not limited to your room, automobile, kitchen, restroom, luggage, writing desk, and footwear. Proceed deliberately and with complete focus on the task at hand. Discard the maximum amount of material feasible.

The majority of individuals harbor a dislike towards the task of cleaning and tend to postpone it until the surroundings have become overwhelmingly untidy. Despite this tendency, it is worth noting that cleaning has been demonstrated to serve as a commendable therapeutic exercise, owing to the emotional bonds that we tend to forge with our possessions. Regular cleaning is an excellent habit as it enables us to eliminate disorder and enhance practicality in the present moment.

Analogous to an untidy kitchen that may give rise to despondency, the mind can potentially suffer from depression due to an overabundance of thoughts. It is important to bear in mind that the addiction to smoking is a deceptive state of mind. The individual who indulges in smoking substances is in fact engrossed in a fictitious world, which prevents them from perceiving reality in its true essence. This can lead to a distorted perception of the present moment. The solitary means of dispelling such unsightly mental disarray is via careful observation, comprehensive comprehension, and judicious mindfulness.

The exercises presented within this book are intended to facilitate the process of mental clarification by eliminating the residue left by smoking habit, thereby enhancing your ability to perceive with clarity. If one has not previously had the opportunity to experience it, the sensation of awakening to a life that is unencumbered by a reliance on cigarettes is one that is invigorating and stimulating.

A period of 15 minutes dedicated to meditative silence and focused respiration. Recite the affirmation: "I am pure." My mental faculties are lucid."

I kindly urge individuals to share their experience using the hashtag #30DaysClean.

Day 24

Exercise:

Please generate a record of pursuits that you have previously embraced but have disregarded, and similarly, craft a compilation of pastimes that you aspire to partake, on a document that facilitates convenient preservation and retrieval for future reference.

Select one hobby that you pursued in the past and another that you aspire to embark on among the given options. I advise your attention to be directed solely towards these two pursuits- the former pastime and the recently acquired one. Make this a priority.

Frequently, individuals have uttered or expressed a desire to pursue a leisure activity but lamented the scarcity of time. However, it is within your capacity to allocate the requisite time for such pursuits. Your perception of time appears to be influenced by the conventional teachings that you have internalized. Given the gravity of the situation, you would undoubtedly prioritize the task at hand, even if it required a significant allocation of your time.

Indeed, time is a human-devised paradigm that should not be ignored. The current moment is the sole existence. The realms of the past and future are not within the present moment. Excessive contemplation regarding time allocation is a prevalent occurrence. What is the frequency of persistent introspective inquiries that revolve around topics such as timing, personal growth, causation, and hypothetical alterations to the past, within your cognitive repertoire?

The act of smoking entails a temporal fixation that could otherwise be redirected towards engaging in leisure pursuits that significantly enhance one's sense of well-being. Consider the potential benefits of cessation of smoking, such as the preservation of valuable time and capital, which may subsequently be allocated toward the cultivation, rekindling, and exploration of personal interests and pastimes.

15 minutes of contemplative and concentrated respiration without verbal or auditory intrusion. Reiterate the maxim: "It is imperative to act promptly". Happiness is present."

Kindly consider sharing your experience by incorporating the hashtag #30DaysHobby.

Day 25

Exercise:

Maintain a facial expression denoting a positive demeanor for a duration of 300 seconds. It is not mandatory to perform this exercise in the presence of a mirror. Nevertheless, you may choose to do so at your discretion. The exercise can be undertaken even within the context of the 15-minute duration of silent and intentful breathing. Whilst maintaining a pleasant facial expression, pause for a moment to consciously perceive the physical sensation of your smile, including the curvature of your lips and cheekbones, by physically touching and feeling them.

Have you ever exhibited a particular behavior and experienced an abrupt shift in your mood? Physical exertion, such as engaging in running or weightlifting, serves this purpose for a considerable number of individuals. Certain types of yoga have additionally been employed by individuals to alter their emotional states. The point is: changing your behavior not only impacts other people, but can also impact your perception of yourself.

It is to be observed that as you engage in this exercise, during the act of smiling, there may arise certain emotional responses. One may experience sensations of discomfort, humiliation, inadequacy, amusement, peculiarity, or similar sentiments. Continue smiling regardless. Similarly, if you are contemplating smoking at this stage of the program, it is suggested that you maintain a positive demeanor by smiling, and retain it until such thoughts dissipate. In case it proves challenging, you may consider setting an alarm reminder to aid the process. Maintain a state of mindfulness while displaying a cheerful countenance. Regard your thoughts with detachment, akin to the procession of clouds traversing a resplendent azure firmament. Efface the negative thoughts with a cheerful disposition.

The act of smiling elicits a genuine physical and mental response within us, which is inherently advantageous. The current juncture is adorned with a pleasant countenance. Kindly maintain that pleasant countenance until such time as it becomes unsustainable.

Fifteen minutes of tranquil contemplation and intentional respiration. Recite the aphorism: "Joyfulness perpetually resides in the present." I am happy."

We kindly invite you to share your experience using the designated hashtag #30DaysSmile.

Section Four: Medical Incentives

41. Nicotine replacement therapy.
NRT is an FDA-approved, non-prescription modality that enables the

consumption of nicotine in a manner distinct from tobacco.

The various forms of NRT encompass adhesive nicotine patches, chewing gums, lozenges, nasal sprays and inhalers.

The utilization of NRT may give rise to certain adverse effects; nevertheless, the perils associated with smoking with regards to one's health are mitigated.

The concomitant utilization of multiple forms of nicotine replacement therapy can potentially augment their efficacy. Based on the statistical evidence, individuals who incorporate this approach in addition to other cessation strategies are more predisposed to successful smoking cessation.

42. E-Cigarettes.

Electronic cigarettes are a form of nicotine replacement therapy and may aid in the alleviation of nicotine withdrawal symptoms.

It aids individuals in cessation efforts by delivering nicotine in a similar fashion as smoking. One noteworthy benefit of an electronic cigarette is its capacity to systematically decrease the concentration of nicotine, while also ensuring that the individual inhales vapor rather than smoke. An additional benefit is derived from the fact that smoking cessation can be achieved while emulating the physical act of smoking.

An added advantage is that the emission of vapor from e-cigarettes does not pose any harm to the individuals in the vicinity, in contrast to the pernicious effects of second-hand cigarette smoke.

43. Prescription medication.

Bupropion and Varenicline are pharmaceuticals that require a prescription and are commonly prescribed to support smoking cessation efforts.

Bupropion is a medication utilized for the treatment of depression, whereas Varenicline is classified as a 'nicotine receptor partial agonist', that is, a substance that triggers a physiological response through the interaction with a receptor.

The potential adverse effects of these medications comprise sleeplessness and queasiness. However, their utilization is limited to a brief duration and restricted to individuals exhibiting severe nicotine addiction.

44. Acupuncture

As a potential complementary approach to assist in the management of nicotine dependence, acupuncture holds promise in alleviating diverse symptoms such as reduced cravings, diminished irritability and anxiety, heightened relaxation, and gradual toxin elimination.

Through the modification of the taste of cigarettes, acupuncture can effectively collaborate with other cessation methods, assisting you in conquering the smoking habit and relinquishing your addiction to nicotine.

45. Acupressure

To alleviate pain without the need for acupuncture, one can employ self-help acupressure techniques that involve massaging specific areas within and near the ears. This gentle manipulation can stimulate the release of endorphins, which possess natural analgesic properties.

46. Hypnosis

As with each and every proposal articulated within this literary piece, it is imperative to exercise prudence by not solely relying on any individual recommendation in isolation. Furthermore, it is essential to conduct a thorough analysis of the potential ramifications of implementing said suggestion with regards to your inclination to cease smoking.

While under hypnosis, a hypnotherapist can propose certain ideas with the aim of diminishing your inclination to smoke. These could include the notion that puffing on a cigarette will result in an exceedingly parched mouth or that the smell of the smoke will resemble that of carbon monoxide exhaust.

It is recommended that individuals consult with their healthcare provider prior to undergoing hypnosis.

Chapter 5: Life Skills Education

47. Out with the old.

Upon your determination to quit smoking, it is highly recommended to dispose of all ashtrays, lighters, and significantly, any remaining cigarettes.

48. Make it memorable.

If the significance of symbolism is paramount to you, why not endeavor to commemorate the disposal of your entire smoking paraphernalia with an unforgettable occasion?

Extend invitations to acquaintances for a social gathering centered on a ceremonial bonfire and consciously dispose of any residual tobacco products.

Please submerge your lighter and any remaining cigarettes into a container of water. Afterwards, kindly place the container into the freezer so that the contents can solidify into a cessation ice block.

Disintegrate your remaining cigarettes into smaller fragments and dispose of them over the precipice.

Implement any and all strategies that may aid in solidifying the notion that this marks the commencement of your journey towards breaking the cycle of smoking addiction.

49. Clean up.

Cleanse your carpets, draperies and furniture, along with any other contaminated items within your dwelling that emit the odor of tobacco smoke. Engage in a purging exercise by either entrusting your vehicle to a valet or meticulously cleaning it on your own.

Eliminate the odor of tobacco smoke from your surroundings. It is possible that you have not previously observed this phenomenon, however, once your nasal passages have begun to clear and recuperate, the scent of stagnant cigarette smoke may become disagreeable to you.

50. Avoid old smoking spots.

Exercise caution in circumstances that may give rise to the temptation to resume smoking. If you have a history of smoking during nightclub outings, it is advisable to refrain from such activities for a period of time, or perhaps consider frequenting establishments where smoking is prohibited on the premises.

If one were accustomed to smoking on a workplace balcony, it would be advisable to refrain from utilizing said balcony and to seek out a different area to obtain fresh air.

51. Shuffle your routine.

If your midday respite typically entails indulging in a caffeinated beverage and tobacco product, may I suggest an alternative course of action involving the consumption of water, tea or juice at least for a temporary period?

If one habitually engages in smoking a cigarette following every meal, it is recommended to consider substituting it with alternatives such as brushing teeth, chewing gum, or consuming a glass of water. According to several studies, it has been indicated that water has a significant impact on the unpleasant taste of cigarettes.

If one is fond of smoking and indulging in television, one may consider opting for a radical alternative by abstaining from viewing.

Engage in stimulating activities such as assembling a jigsaw puzzle, adopting a fitness regimen, or delving into a literary work. If you find it challenging to relinquish both smoking and indulging in television, consider substituting your smoking habit with a serving of fresh fruit or bowl of popcorn.

If an individual has developed a habitual practice of smoking in their automobile during their regular commute, specific locations or rest stops can potentially elicit a craving to smoke. A recommended approach to discontinuing this behavior is to alter one's route of transportation and take an alternate path to the workplace.

52. Break the physical habit.

Furthermore, smoking can be regarded as a repetitive physical behavior in addition to being an addictive habit. Hence, it is a complex interdependence. Breaking the habit is imperative for overcoming the addiction.

Perceive it not, whether the preponderance of recommendations mentioned in the book pertains to smoking behavior, and not solely to nicotine addiction?

Ceasing the repetitive action of raising one's hand to the mouth may not appear significant in the present moment; nevertheless, this is the very manifestation of indulging in smoking.

To overcome this addiction, it may be necessary to engage in alternative activities that can keep your hands and mouth occupied for a certain period of time.

It can be likened to the experience of transitioning from a manual gear-change transmission vehicle to an automobile equipped with an automatic transmission, after having used the former for several years. During the upcoming weeks, your attention will be directed towards locating the clutch and gear lever.

53. Keep your hands busy.

Take hold of a writing instrument, such as a pen or pencil, and if it facilitates the process, you may simulate smoking it.

Engage in the activity of manipulating an elastic band or a series of interconnected paper clips.

Manipulate a fiber cord ornamented with spherical objects.

Acquire a stress-relief ball to compress and manipulate, or produce one yourself by inserting baking flour into a balloon.

54. Reprogram your mind.

Your brain has undergone a process of conditioning in which it has associated the act of smoking with specific temporal, spatial, and contextual cues that occur throughout your daily routine. When an opportunity arises at any of these given instances or locations, you shall inevitably develop an inclination to ignite.

Allow yourself to confront and surmount every instance, location, and occurrence, thereby transforming your mindset while attaining a triumph of the psyche. One should embrace the recuperation that follows after successfully overcoming every challenge.

55. Discover novel approaches to alleviate stress and recuperate.

Smoking potentially served as a coping mechanism for managing the stresses and demands inherent in one's daily routine.

Upon cessation of smoking, it is vital to acknowledge that one's lifestyle and daily pressures are unlikely to transform. As such, it becomes crucial to explore alternative avenues to alleviate stress and tension.

A manifest channel for dissipating adverse energy is to engage in physical activity and engage in exercise. Engaging in physical activity can effectively reduce the urge to consume nicotine and alleviate associated withdrawal symptoms. Various forms of physical exercise such as jogging or gardening can serve as a healthful outlet.

In addition to engaging in physical activities, there exist numerous other activities that facilitate the reduction of stress.

Broaden your range of interests to unearth a previously undiscovered aspect of your persona.

Initiate a novel recreational pursuit such as enrolling in culinary courses, acquiring painting skills, commencing a produce garden, or obtaining a domestic animal companion, whether it be a puppy, kitten, or any other species of your preference.

56. This too shall pass.

The indomitable spirit of mankind endows us with a remarkable ability to bounce back from adversity.

You have exhibited a commendable sense of dedication and fortitude in making the choice to cease smoking, which is indicative of your ability to triumph over challenges and rise above impediments.

The prospects for improvement in life are promising from this point onwards.

57. Breathe.

Kindly refrain from disregarding the significance of this particular advice due to its seemingly trivial nature. Rather, do take a moment to engage in conscious breathing for optimal outcomes.

Inhale deeply to take in a sufficient amount of fresh air and subsequently exhale to release it from your lungs. Are you sensing the expanding and contracting motions within your lungs? They represent an essential component of human existence.

Your commendable resolve to cease smoking has afforded a renewed lease of life to your respiratory organs.

When experiencing overpowering urges and signs of withdrawal, take a moment to center yourself by inhaling and exhaling deeply.

On a daily basis, commencing from the day in which one quits smoking, the respiratory organs initiate the process of recuperating themselves- inhale.

Inhale deeply and exhale gradually, acknowledging and cherishing each nourishing breath.

58. Laugh.

Derive as much mirth from your existence as you inhale and exhale.

Your decision is one that will yield positive outcomes for the remainder of your life.

With the abstinence of nicotine, every passing day shall witness the body's self-healing and detoxification. It is likely that your olfactory and gustatory senses will experience enhancements. Respiration is anticipated to become less challenging. It is anticipated that your cardiovascular parameters will reach a state of equilibrium. Your overall state of wellness is expected to enhance. I must express my admiration for your exceptional achievements and commendable efforts, as they are undoubtedly noteworthy and truly deserving of recognition.

59. Prayer and meditation.

Directing one's attention towards a higher purpose or objective can assist in gaining a broader understanding of one's circumstances. Given our inherent fallibility as human beings, we may rely on the intervention of divine forces to reinforce our resilience amidst moments of adversity.

Coughing Up Blood

I found myself hunched over the sink, unable to maintain bodily composure. My eyesight gradually receded from the periphery, attaining ultimate dimness until I could discern nothing except a couple of focal points and the basin in my vicinity.

After the coughing abated and I glanced downwards, an ample amount of blood was discernible in the basin. As I peered into the reflective surface, my eyes, reddened, fixated on the scene behind me. I observed my toddler daughter gazing at me with curiosity, perhaps pondering about the cause of her father's distress.

Throughout the entirety of my life, and in advance of her existence, I had engaged in the habit of smoking. Her complete characterization of my persona was rooted in my consumption of a cigarette at the outset of each day, after every meal, and intermittently throughout the day.

As I witnessed the quivering of my daughter's lip reflected in the mirror, it dawned upon me that some modifications were imperative.

I had attempted to cease the habit previously through various methods. On certain occasions, my decision to discontinue persisted for a period spanning several months, or in some cases, even a year. During the majority of the decade encompassing my twenties, I perceived myself not as a smoker per se, but rather as an individual who indulged in smoking sporadically at his own discretion, and who believed he could do so without succumbing to nicotine dependency.

For an extended duration, I possessed the capability to control smoking. However, on that morning, it became apparent to me that there had been a significant shift. The locus of control had shifted from my agency to the influence of cigarettes. As I gazed into the apprehensive eyes of my offspring, a moment of epiphany dawned upon me, signifying the gravity of the situation. Today is the day. If I do not discontinue my current pursuits at present, probability suggests that I may never discontinue them in the future. Furthermore, it dawned on me that in the event of a subsequent failure to abstain, my resolve would be forever compromised.

Regrettably, my grandmother passed away while occupying a hospital bed while holding a cigarette. Regrettably, my uncle passed away at a relatively young age of sixty-something as a result of being unable to break free from the aforementioned addiction. Each evening, it was necessary for him to slumber with a mechanical respiratory device to sustain his vital functions. On a daily basis, as soon as his spouse averted her gaze, he would surreptitiously venture outdoors to indulge in an additional cigarette. He was aware of the fact that his life was being extinguished, yet he remained powerless to prevent its cessation.

Tobacco usage was unfortunately a detrimental legacy in my family history, which I am determined to refrain from perpetuating by any means, particularly in regards to my beloved daughter.

Does this narrative evoke personal resonance?

In the event of such circumstances, let us contemplate the actuality of the experience of being a smoker, as well as the enduring consequences of perpetuating this detrimental practice.

Benefits Of Giving Up Smoking For Your Health And Mental Well-Being

According to the CDC, smoking is a prominent contributor to numerous afflictions and illnesses, which not only curtail one's lifespan but also diminish the standard of living. Allow me to present a few pertinent points to bear in mind with regard to the issue of nicotine dependence:

The majority of individuals who smoke develop a dependence on nicotine, which is an inherent component of tobacco.

Nicotine is the most widely abused substance in the United States, with a higher prevalence of addiction compared to all other drugs.

According to research, nicotine exhibits similar addictive properties as those observed in heroin, cocaine, and alcohol.

Cessation of smoking is a formidable challenge and may necessitate multiple attempts.

Individuals who cease cigarette smoke consumption frequently relapse due to the manifestation of withdrawal symptoms, heightened levels of stress, and an increased propensity towards weight gain.

Manifestations of nicotine abstention may encompass:

Experiencing irritability, anger, or anxiety.

Having trouble thinking

Craving tobacco products

Feeling hungrier than usual

Fortunately, there is also some good news about nicotine dependence. Cessation of smoking is correlated with the ensuing advantages to one's health:

The incidence of various cancer types, such as lung cancer, has been observed to decrease significantly.

The likelihood of developing heart disease, stroke, and peripheral vascular disease, characterized by constriction of blood vessels outside the heart, is diminished.

The likelihood of developing cardiovascular disorders is comparatively lower after abstaining from smoking for a period of one to two years.

The prevalence of respiratory symptoms, such as coughing, wheezing, and breathlessness, has decreased. Although cessation of smoking may not alleviate these symptoms completely, it does impede their further progression in contrast to persistent smoking.

There is a decreased probability of experiencing certain respiratory ailments (such as chronic obstructive pulmonary disease, which is acknowledged as a primary cause of mortality in the United States).

Diminished likelihood of infertility in females within the reproductive age bracket. Women who abstain from smoking during the gestational period can also mitigate their chances of delivering a neonate with significantly decreased body mass.

The Pragmatic Advantages of Cessation of Smoking Habits in Reality

The aforementioned bullet points and facts do not provide a comprehensive portrayal of the experience of smoking cessation. Let us delve into the potential outcomes that may arise upon cessation of this habitual activity.

Presented herewith are some prompt advantages you shall encounter:

Upon cessation of smoking, the cardiac rhythm returns to its baseline level within twenty minutes.

Within a span of merely twelve hours, the level of carbon monoxide entrenched within your bloodstream regresses to a customary level.

Within a mere span of two weeks, a decrease in the probability of experiencing a cardiac arrest and a significant enhancement in pulmonary capabilities is observed.

During the initial nine-month period, a gradual reduction in coughing and breathlessness shall be observed. Each respiration you undertake will result in a heightened sense of satisfaction and improved respiratory experience. After a year of cessation, you may be pleasantly surprised by the significant augmentation in the amount of oxygen that your bloodstream can assimilate.

This is the pace at which one can commence witnessing remarkable outcomes.

In a span of five to fifteen years, your probability of experiencing a stroke reduces to that of an individual who has never engaged in smoking, while your likelihood of developing cancer (with particular emphasis on the mouth, throat, and esophagus) cuts down by fifty percent compared to that of a smoker.

After a decade of quitting smoking, the likelihood of succumbing to lung, bladder, cervical or pancreatic cancer is halved in comparison to the dangers faced when smoking.

Ultimately, after a period of fifteen years subsequent to cessation, your probability of experiencing a cardiac event is equivalent to that of a non-smoker.

In addition to the aforementioned enduring advantages, albeit difficult to envision one's emotional state in the span of fifteen years, there exist remarkable supplementary benefits:

#1: Quality of life. As an individual with a habit of chronic smoking, I would require a cigarette to achieve a sense of normalcy. I always felt a step behind. I incurred frequent illnesses. I have suffered from pneumonia and bronchitis for almost twenty occasions over the course of my life. However, since quitting smoking, I have not encountered any such instances so far.

On a certain occasion, whilst taking a stroll towards the main entrance, I recollected that I had inadvertently left an item in our bedroom situated on the highest floor. I stated, "May I have a moment of your time to share a thought? Forget it. It appears that the distance between us is comparable to that of being situated on opposite sides of a mountain. The distance is considerably vast, which is rather surprising as I remember conveniently surpassing one or even two steps while ascending or descending between classes during my high school years. Presently, the prospect of ascending and descending a staircase transformed into a source of immense apprehension.

One of the paramount advantages of cessation is experiencing an improved state of well-being. You no longer perceive an imminent proximity of demise towards your physical being. Conversely, you may experience heightened vitality even as you approach your third, fourth, and fifth decades of life. It is akin to reclaiming certain aspects of one's youth.

#2: Health. Beyond just feeling better, you will actually be better. Having successfully overcome my dependency on nicotine, my frequency of doctor visits has markedly decreased. Over the course of the preceding year, each member comprising my family, with the exception of myself, has been required to receive medical attention in a hospital setting. Despite being senior in age compared to my spouse and offspring, I am currently in the most optimal state of physiological well-being. It is a pleasant experience to visit the dental practitioner without apprehension of eliciting a negative response due to the odorous emanations from my oral cavity. It gives me a sense of relief to visit the physician's clinic without apprehension of elevated blood pressure that could necessitate the use of potentially hazardous medication.

#3: The smell. Upon cessation of smoking, I observed a conspicuous foul odor emanating from unwashed clothes and certain areas of my dwelling. The olfactory senses of a smoker are profoundly affected, leading to their inability to perceive the unpleasant odor associated with tobacco smoke. Upon cessation, an individual becomes cognizant of the unpleasant odor and flavor emanating from their person. I am unsure how my spouse could withstand the act of kissing me despite my breath being reminiscent of an ashtray. She is no longer required to endure the said predicament.

#4: The cost. The cost of cigarettes can range from $5 to $15 in various locations. That cumulatively increases as time passes.

Perform the necessary calculations: If one consumes a pack of cigarettes on a daily basis, the expenditure would amount to no less than $35 per week. In the lower echelons of the pricing spectrum, one can expect to pay approximately $120 per month, translating to an annual expenditure of roughly $1,500. What potential opportunities do you envision for yourself if you were to come into possession of an additional $1,500? Currently, I have the means to afford weekly movie outings with my family, wherein the cost of tickets and even certain refreshments is lower than that of my smoking habit. Furthermore, this activity yields greater enjoyment and satisfaction.

#5: A proud family. My spouse and offspring were appalled as they observed me engaging in smoking and experiencing fits of cough accompanied by discharge of blood. Not only were we incurring expenses on tobacco products, but also on medical treatments and hospitalizations. The various elements were cumulatively combining to form a coherent picture. At present, they hold a sense of pride towards me. They express profound enthusiasm regarding my success in overcoming the habit of smoking and my current role as a mentor, guiding others in their journey towards the same achievement.

#6: Skin. I distinctly recollect an episode of the classic TV comedy Seinfeld, wherein Kramer endeavors to convert his apartment into a domicile for smokers, owing to the prohibition of smoking at any other location. Soon thereafter, Kramer's epidermis acquires a leathery texture, owing to the deleterious effects of excessive exposure to cigarette smoke. While the statement errs on the side of hyperbole, there is indeed some truth to it.

Prior to sensing an individual's scent, one may observe their hands and skin to ascertain their tobacco usage. Their digits display a yellow tinge indicative of nicotine accumulation, and their complexion exhibits an unhealthy, pallid hue. Subsequent to my cessation of smoking, I was astounded to discover that individuals perceived me to be a decade younger.

The prospect of having an extended lifespan and witnessing the maturation of one's progeny is a compelling reason to aspire towards longevity. Undoubtedly, this represents the most significant advantage for me. The prospect of being deprived of witnessing my daughter's high school graduation, her initiation into a career, or her experience of love fills me with immense dread. I derive immense satisfaction from the realization that I have effectively improved the probabilities in my favor. I am certain that I will be present to witness the arrival of my grandchildren and, optimistically, even my great-grandchildren. I earnestly wish that my grandmother were present to meet my children. I lament the absence of my dearly cherished uncle, with whom I shared a close bond, to witness the growth of my offspring and pay me a visit. It is a disconcerting thought to contemplate his exclusion from that experience, not to mention his inability to meet his own descendants. It is lamentable that my children need not endure the ill-effects of smoking any longer.

Cease all forms of public criticism and evaluation. It's come full circle. Previously, individuals regarded me with disdain and repulsion, whereas presently, I have adopted a comparable perception towards individuals who smoke. My aversion towards smoking, despite having no ill will towards those who engage in it, assists me in avoiding its allure. I am not obliged to resist the inclination to engage in smoking. I've killed that desire.

The sense of servitude that was once experienced has dissipated. I recall one of my esteemed companions during college who displayed a dependence on cigarettes, to the extent that their morning routine entailed smoking a cigarette before getting out of bed. In the past, he would habitually position an ash receptacle in close proximity to his bedding, subsequently recline with a lit cigarette in hand, and proceed to smoke exhaust fumes directly above his cushion. Such was the minimal level of self-control exerted by him. His daily routine was incomplete unless he indulged in his morning cigar.

I can empathize with the experience of feeling helpless. I recollect harboring the thought of relinquishing my endeavors on multiple occasions. I used to consume half a pack of cigarettes and feel inclined to justify its use to myself. Despite my attempts to quit smoking between packs, I faced difficulty in doing so. I am now able to exercise my own volition once more. I am experiencing a sensation of liberation that had eluded me for a significant period of time.

#10: Sports and fitness. During the nadir of my physical condition, I gazed into my reflection and articulated, "Dear self, it appears that ascending even a single flight of stairs without experiencing a rapid cardiac rhythm and undue respiratory strain akin to that of 'The Big Bad Wolf' from 'The Three Little Pigs' is an unattainable feat. Regrettably, the prospect of running in the foreseeable future is unattainable, and acknowledging that my feet remain firmly planted on the earth plane is an inevitability." It is deemed highly improbable that you shall be indulged with the opportunity to take a leap in the future." At the dawn of my thirties, I had already relinquished three integral facets of my existence.

After the elapse of a quinquennium, I engage in training sessions of kickboxing under the tutelage of a seasoned pugilist for a period of five days each week. I am currently executing jumping, spinning kicks and delivering elbow strikes, engaging in a sprint, performing jumping jacks and executing push-ups. I do it all. Previously, each of my daily activities resided on my overlooked or neglected roster. It is indeed a gratifying experience to engage in all the activities that brought me joy during my high school years and confidently declare that I need not abandon them.

Age is not a determining factor, regardless of whether one is in their fifties, sixties or seventies. When you decide to forego smoking, you can embark on a journey towards regaining optimal health and physical fitness. One may consider increasing the pace of their gait, subsequently transitioning to a jog, thus eventually making cycling a viable option once more.

It is comparatively effortless to respire. Your perception is not unfounded. Upon cessation of smoking, within the initial year, the physiological process of lung purification and enhanced bodily efficiency shall transpire. With each inhalation, a greater volume of air shall be ingested, thereby enhancing the proportion of oxygen converted per respiratory cycle. I have personally experienced the sensation of being breathless, however, I am proud to say that it is now a past recollection. I am proficient in jogging, running, and sprinting, and my respiratory capacity does not act as a hindrance. Previously, my respiratory organs had restrained me to the earth, but presently they have evolved to lift me towards the heights.

#12: More energy. Regrettably, within our current societal context, the inclination is to resort to chemical-based solutions as a panacea to address multifaceted challenges.

Are you experiencing difficulty in arising in the morning? Consume a serving of coffee.

Are you experiencing a sense of low spirits or despondency? Smoke a cigarette.

Feeling lonely? Drink some alcohol.

That is excluding the discussion on non-prescription pharmaceuticals. Previously, I harbored the belief that energy originated from chemical reactions. Consuming dubious energy beverages and tobacco smoking aided me in coping with my extended work sessions, while I crafted my initial literary works and established my business enterprise. Presently, as I abstain from smoking, my energy reserves remain consistently high. Each day, I promptly arise between the hours of 4:00 and 5:00 a.m. without prompting from an alarm, owing to my innate readiness to commence the day.

You'll be amazed at how much energy is unlocked when you can fully access your lungs, and your blood begins to pump oxygen-filled hemoglobin through your body at maximum efficiency. Indeed, it has become commonplace for us to resort to the use of cigarettes and other chemical substances as coping mechanisms. However, this only serves to perpetuate a cycle of dependency and reliance, ultimately replacing one issue with another. Upon resolving the root cause, you shall unveil an exquisite reserve of vitality dwelling within your physique, awaiting emancipation.

#13: Lower stress. The paradoxical aspect of smoking is that it is commonly perceived as a means to alleviate stress. This was one of the most common responses we received when Steve and I polled our audiences: we need cigarettes to lower stress. However, it can be observed that cigarettes exhibit antithetical properties. They solely induce a placebo response.

The principal indicator of stress is the level of blood pressure, and the act of smoking escalates the level of blood pressure. Following the cessation of my smoking habit, I have encountered only a single occurrence of elevated blood pressure. I underwent a physical examination three years prior. Due to the elevated nature of my blood pressure, the medical personnel recommended strong medication for its management. I had requested to conduct the test once again before proceeding, stating, 'Prior to engaging in the activity, let us run the test again.' Upon executing the test for a second time, I deliberately closed my eyes. I consciously induced a state of relaxation, which facilitated my attainment of a flawless score. As a preventative measure, I opted to purchase a blood pressure monitoring device from a nearby pharmacy. I subject myself to self-examination on a weekly basis, and over the last two years, my blood pressure has remained consistently stable. As per the foremost stress indicator, my well-being can be considered satisfactory.

After careful consideration of our intimate experiences, I must say that your abilities in the bedroom are exceptional. The presence of nicotine in the body, in conjunction with elevated blood pressure and detrimental effects on the vascular system due to smoking, constitute predominant factors in the onset of erectile dysfunction. Allow me to enlighten you that the cessation of smoking, regardless of one's gender, typically leads to a significant enhancement in sexual capabilities.

#15: Fertility. Upon quitting smoking, my spouse and I have observed that on every occasion we have decided to expand our family, conception has occurred expeditiously on the initial attempt. If that phenomenon does not pertain to fecundity, I am uncertain of its classification.

#16: Eliminate secondhand smoke. Due to the presence of my young child during that period of time when I engaged in significant smoking, it was imperative for me to relocate outside and utilize a small ledge adjacent to the window in order to smoke. Amidst my acquaintances from secondary education, it has been observed that individuals whose parents indulged in smoking exhibit the most pronounced issues with cigarette addiction presently. Regardless of one's confidence in the messages conveyed by the advertisements during the nineties concerning the risks attributed to secondhand smoke, it is imperative to acknowledge the fact that being in proximity to parental smoking can significantly impact an individual's health and well-being. It significantly enhances the probability of adopting smoking as a personal habit. I prefer not to have such circumstances for my offspring.

#17: Cholesterol. Tobacco consumption serves as a harbinger for various illnesses. It not only elevates your blood pressure levels, but also augments your cholesterol levels and engenders occlusions in your circulatory system. There's a reason science points to such a tight correlation between smoking and heart attacks. An optimistic development is that upon abstaining from smoking, the likelihood of encountering a heart attack decreases promptly, and the levels of cholesterol begin to adjust towards normalcy.

The condition of having diminished blood viscosity and the associated risk of thrombotic events. Furthermore, apart from other detrimental effects, it has been discovered that smoking engenders a susceptibility to the formation and subsequent dislodgment of a blood clot, which is capable of obstructing vital arteries leading to fatal consequences in the heart, brain or lungs. As if tobacco usage wasn't already deleterious and pernicious to one's health through a multitude of mechanisms.

#19: Hypertension. Hypertension is a medical terminology employed to denote the physiological condition of elevated arterial blood pressure. Upon examination of the top ten leading causes of fatality among Americans, it has been determined that a staggering six of them stem from the presence of hypertension. The act of smoking does not result in immediate fatality. Consumption of this material may lead to hypertension and result in detrimental impact on your overall health.

Moreover, ceasing the habit of smoking yields remarkable advantages, including a preventive measure against auditory and ocular impairment. Enhanced bone density, muscular strength, and immune system function are among the benefits, along with expedited wound healing.

The Dangers of Inaction

We have just discussed the manifold health advantages that come with abstaining from smoking. Allow me to provide a succinct depiction of the experience of succumbing to a state of inactivity.

I live on the beach. Currently, I am situated on a pier, verbally composing this chapter amidst the undulating movements of the ocean waves. The shoreline imparts a significant lesson upon us. If I remain stationary with my feet submerged in the sand and water, my body does not maintain a state of rest. Upon the arrival of each successive wave, as it collides with my feet, I find myself gradually drawn further and further into the boundless expanse of the ocean. If I remain stationary for a prolonged duration, it is probable that I'll be gradually drawn towards the vast ocean and eventually find myself stranded in its midst.

Passivity cannot be equated to stillness. Merely refraining from taking action at present does not signify that no progress or development is taking place. With each passing day that you defer the act of quitting smoking, the state of your health deteriorates gradually and takes you one step away from achieving your goals.

On every occasion that you express statements such as "Not yet," "I am not prepared," or "It is beyond my abilities," you distance yourself incrementally from accomplishing success. The more you procrastinate, the greater the erosion of your self-belief, culminating in a complete disillusionment of your inner strength and resolve.

Moreover, there has been a steady decline in your physical well-being. Every instance of smoking a cigarette significantly reduces an individual's lifespan, which is a well-documented fact. It appears that your intention for reading this book is not driven by the query on the ill effects of smoking. The reason you are perusing this literary work is to discover a source of motivation and guidance towards emancipation.

The ultimate and gravest consequence of failing to take action is the possibility of transmitting this to your offspring. Consider the potential of your decision to smoke and how it may impact not only your own reputation, but also that of your offspring in the years to come.

We have extensively discussed the advantages of cessation and the efficacy of abandoning the smoking habit. It is important to note that the aforementioned details are not being enumerated merely for informational purposes; rather, they are intended to instill a sense of inspiration in you and ignite your enthusiasm towards the cessation process. Contemplating such diverse rationales before you serves to invigorate and compel you.

Presently, it is opportune to transition from ideation to execution. This literary work entails content beyond the cessation of smoking. This literary work serves as a practical manual oriented towards fostering productive behaviour. This entails a systematic approach aimed at implementing a set of measures to culminate in the positive outcome of eliminating smoking from your life.

Reflection Questions

Which of the health benefits from the CDC can you most connect to? May I inquire if you are experiencing anticipation regarding the emotions you shall experience within the next fifteen minutes, a year, or fifteen years?

May I inquire as to which among the myriad advantages enumerated and the anecdotes I have recounted from my personal experiences strikes a chord with you?

Did any of these advantages come as a surprise to you, or were you previously unaware of them?

May I inquire as to whether you have experienced any of the aforementioned issues? Have you ever experienced a non-healing injury? Have you experienced any respiratory complications? Have you frequently experienced any ailments? Did someone issue a disparaging remark concerning your complexion?

Are you currently feeling enthused about embarking on this journey with us and engaging in collaboration with an individual who has experienced circumstances similar to yours, an individual who possesses firsthand knowledge and has successfully overcome them?

Your Action Plan

Select the most significant advantage that aligns with your values and objectives, and proceed to develop a visual representation of it through the creation of a vision board. Locate imagery and affix it onto a sheet of mounting paper. You are required to conceive a prospective vision for your future where the aforementioned advantage shall be the focal point of your existence.

This poster board shall serve as a source of inspiration for you. It is imperative that you place your personal vision for the future in a location where it would be visible to you constantly.

Affix it to the upper part of your bedroom's ceiling, such that it becomes the ultimate image in your consciousness before you retire to bed and the first one to encounter upon awakening, thereby serving as a constant reminder of the purpose behind your endeavor.

Despite the occasional temporary discomfort, you can view that board and affirm, "That is the lifestyle I desire." That is a prospective outcome which aligns with my aspirations."

Allocate a considerable amount of time towards the development and construction of your vision board. Once the item is prepared to your satisfaction and suitably mounted on the wall, kindly accompany me into the subsequent chapter.

Reflection Questions

May I inquire as to which of these methods you have attempted previously and encountered obstacles?

What is the chief obstacle impeding your cessation efforts?

What is your primary apprehension concerning the cessation process?

Upon a comprehensive examination of these various methods, may I inquire as to your opinion on what, in your estimation, could be identified as the most significant drawback?

What is the underlying reason for the lack of efficacy of these methods for a significant number of individuals, while proving successful for only a particular subset of the population?

Your Action Plan

As we proceed with the execution phase of this book, our attention will be primarily directed towards implementation, as the responsibility now lies with you to take affirmative action. To commence the proceedings, we shall be undertaking a shared activity.

It is commonly referred to as the "one-day cessation" technique.

In essence, you shall refrain from smoking entirely for a period of twenty-four hours, commencing immediately.

This implies that upon awakening tomorrow, you will refrain from smoking until such time as you have had the opportunity to rest once again. We shall embark on a twenty-four-hour cessation regimen, subsequent to which we shall meticulously evaluate each phase of the procedure. As you traverse through this journey, it is expected that you will maintain a comprehensive record of your entire encounter.

There are individuals who have a strong inclination to smoke a cigarette as their first act of the day. Some individuals may require it immediately following a meal, in times of heightened stress, or during their daily commute. Our intention is to compile an inventory and formulate a comprehensive strategy based on your behavior patterns, in order to identify each of your smoking stimuli. We shall utilize this catalogue subsequently, to further tailor our habit stacking scheme for the substitution of your smoking inclination.

Please keep in mind that this initial stage is solely the beginning of a more comprehensive process, rather than the conclusive one.

In the event of an inadvertent relapse during lunchtime, endeavor to abstain from smoking for the remainder of the day. Please evaluate and assign a rank to each instance of craving or trigger that you experience, and subsequently determine the degree of difficulty associated with it by assessing it on a scale ranging from one to ten. If an individual succumbs to the temptation of smoking a cigarette, it would undoubtedly result in a rating of ten. The intensity of the inclination was so potent that it overcame your volition. That's OK. Our primary focus is to identify and isolate the most potent triggers, and address them initially while progressing through this undertaking.

Dedicate a sufficient amount of time towards journal writing as a means to deeply acquaint oneself. Abstaining from smoking for a day can reveal hitherto unknown triggers that might have escaped your notice. Upon completion of this procedure, kindly proceed towards the subsequent chapter alongside me.

www.ingramcontent.com/pod-product-compliance
Lightning Source LLC
Chambersburg PA
CBHW050028130526
44590CB00042B/2042